BEANS & PEAS

Beautifully cooked beans or peas count among the most delectable of vegetables, and here is a fine array of recipes for all types—from limas to lentils, from fava beans to snow peas. Exciting new recipes for such delights as "Green Pea Soufflé" (a savory main dish), "Green Beans with Hazelnut Sauce" (an accompaniment for poultry) and "Shell Bean Chakee" (an incredible vegetable curry) are included here with a wide range of accompaniments to suit any taste, meal, or mood.

secrets of vegetable cooking

. . . is a series of attractive, low-priced cookbooks, each concerned with a specific vegetable and, most important, each containing a collection of more than 50 distinctive and delicious recipes for the broadest range of vegetable dishes. A special treat—the soup to nuts of vegetable cookery.

Inez M. Krech, author of the entire series, is well known as a writer (she was the co-author of "Naturally Italian") and as the editor of more than 200 cookbooks. She lives in New Jersey.

BEANS & PEAS

by inez m. krech

primavera books crown publishers, inc. / new york

secrets of vegetable cooking

Inquiries should be addressed to
Crown Publishers, Inc., One Park Avenue, New York, New York 10016

Printed in the United States of America

Published simultaneously in
Canada by General Publishing Company Limited

Library of Congress Cataloging in Publication Data

Krech, Inez M.
   Beans & peas.

   (Secrets of vegetable cooking)
   1. Cookery (Beans) 2. Cookery (Peas) I. Title.
II. Title: Beans and peas. III. Series: Krech, Inez M.
Secrets of vegetable cooking.
TX803.B4K66 1981   641.6'565   81-7839
ISBN 0-517-54446-6   AACR2

10 9 8 7 6 5 4 3 2 1
First edition

DESIGN AND COVER PHOTOGRAPH BY ALBERT SQUILLACE

Introduction

Peas and beans are legumes, seeds of plants with blossoms like sweet-pea flowers. This enormous group of plants, with thousands of species, includes such diverse kinds as clovers and other fodder plants, peanuts, lima beans, lentils, chick-peas. In all of these plants the seeds develop in pods which split open along the two lengthwise seams when the seeds are mature. When the pods are immature and tender, the whole thing can be eaten; snap beans and snow peas are good examples. Some have tough pods even when immature, and these are always shelled; the pod is discarded and only the seeds are eaten; lima beans and black-eyed peas are typical.

With the exception of snow peas, in which the seeds remain tiny and soft, all the peas and beans used for human food can be shelled, like green peas and limas, to make fresh shell beans. These include cranberry beans, black-eyed peas (also called white peas and cow peas, especially in Southern states), rice beans (very small and tender), fava or broad beans (very large beans), lima beans, flageolets (like miniature limas, pale green and tender), white beans and both red and white kidney beans. Most of these beans, as well as green and yellow peas, brown beans, black beans, chick-peas, soybeans, mung beans, etc., are more familiar to us as dried beans. In dried form these peas and beans serve to nourish countless humans, for they can be stored for relatively long times and are extremely nutritious when rehydrated and cooked, even more so when sprouted. But this book deals only with fresh peas and beans.

Green peas, fresh, canned or frozen, are extremely nutritious, providing large amounts of amino acids, fair amounts of minerals, especially potassium, and B vitamins. Like all legumes, they are relatively high in calories; there are about 70 calories in 100 grams (about 3-1/2 ounces) of cooked peas. Snow peas, with their tiny immature seeds, are less caloric, about 40 calories in 100 grams of cooked snow peas.

Snap beans, green or yellow, provide 20 to 30 calories per 100 grams cooked, fewer calories than peas because the seeds are still tiny and immature. But these too are very nutritious, providing amino acids, minerals and vitamins, particularly vitamin A; green snap beans are a very good source of A. Canned and frozen beans are almost as nutritious.

Lima beans and fava or broad beans are both caloric and nutritious. When cooked 100 grams provide at least 110 calories along with large amounts of amino acids, some minerals, especially potassium, and vitamins. Canned and frozen beans are also rich in these nutrients.

4

Other shell beans have varied caloric value, but generally about 1 calorie per gram, and all provide amino acids, minerals, especially potassium, and some vitamins. The good content of amino acids in all these legumes, even in the fresh state, makes them especially valuable for vegetarians or for those who have a limited meat supply for other reasons.

Fresh Peas

Some fresh peas can be found during most of the year, but the chief season is spring and early summer. Buy only those with crisp shiny pods. While a fat pod may not contain fat peas, you can be sure of finding only tiny soft peas in flat pods. Refrigerate them until ready to use; they will keep for about 3 days. Shell just before using. To have 2 cups shelled peas, buy 2 pounds in the pod. This will give you 4 servings alone, more combined with other ingredients. For some recipes you may want to save a few pods to add flavor.

If you grow your own peas, you can freeze any excess crop. Use only perfect peas. Shell and wash them, then blanch them, 2 cups at a time, in boiling water for 1-1/2 minutes, longer if the peas are very large. Drain, cool in ice water, drain again, then pour into containers and freeze. When solidly frozen, seal or overwrap and label.

Edible-Podded Peas

These delicate green morsels are most often associated with Oriental cooking, but they were grown in English home gardens over fifty years ago. They are now commonly called "snow peas" although the terms "Chinese peas" and "sugar peas" are also used. The pod is flat, with barely developed peas inside, and the whole thing is eaten. Store them covered in the refrigerator, but plan to use them within 2 days after purchase. These peas are a very expensive vegetable, often sold in tiny packages of 2 or 3 ounces, so they are seldom served as a vegetable alone but rather in combination with others, or as part of a meat or poultry dish.

When you are ready to cook the peas, wash them, top and tail them as you would a fresh snap bean, and gently pull off the strings on either side of the pod. Sometimes this causes the pod to separate.

Lacking fresh peas, frozen can substitute for appearance, but the texture is not as crisp and they are not as flavorful. Also, it is impossible to string them while still frozen; if peas are defrosted before cooking they become mushy. Frozen peas are sometimes found in combination with other vegetables, especially bamboo shoots and other Chinese favorites.

If you grow your own, pick them when quite small (commercial peas are about 3 inches long). To freeze them, sort and wash them, but do not cut off tips or string them. Bring a large pot of water to a boil. Place about 1 pound of the peas in a steamer basket or cheesecloth bag and lower them into the boiling water. As soon as the water returns to a boil, count 1 minute, then lift out the basket or bag and at once cool in ice water. Drain, pat dry, package, and freeze. When solidly frozen, seal or overwrap and label.

Snap Beans

Once upon a time we had a bean called a "string bean" and it did have strings, one along each side of the pod. When preparing these for cooking, it was necessary to pull off the strings. Lots of work by botanists has resulted in a stringless bean, generally called "snap bean." When you break one of these beans, it makes a loud snap. If it doesn't snap, the bean is no longer fresh and it will be less nutritious and less flavorful. Green beans are available all year long, but very expensive in winter months. They are best in late spring to early fall, and of course best when fresh. Store them in the refrigerator, covered; they will still be edible after a week, but for really good beans cook and eat within 3 days. Buy 1 pound for 4 average servings.

Yellow snap beans, or wax beans, are available during summer and early fall. They are treated in the same ways as the green ones.

If you grow your own, in bush or pole form, you will have beans by the hundreds all at once. To keep the vines producing, pick them at once and freeze or pickle the excess. For shell beans, leave the pods on the vine until they are beginning to dry. Gather them, shell them, store in refrigerator, and cook within 2 days.

To freeze fresh snap beans, wash them, top and tail them, and blanch in boiling water for 3 minutes. Drain beans, chill in ice water, drain again, package, and freeze. Seal and label.

Lima Beans

Once these were available fresh in all country markets, but they are so difficult to shell that now most of the crop is frozen. The time required for the beans to reach maturity is long, which means that these fresh beans are almost unknown in northern areas (Canada knows them as frozen or canned beans). A late summer and early fall treat. Buy at least 2 pounds for 4 servings, for the shells are almost half of the weight. Use kitchen scissors or a sharp knife to cut a slice down the side of each pod, pry the pod open, and push the beans out. But shell only when you are ready to cook them; they lose flavor if stored after shelling.

To freeze baby limas, follow directions for green peas, but blanch the large (Fordhook) limas for 4 to 5 minutes.

Fava or Broad Beans

These are available frozen under the name "Italian beans." My English friends who grow these gather only 2 or 3 individual beans per serving, as the beans in pods are so large. Usually they cut the pods into 1- or 2-inch diagonal pieces and cook them like any snap bean. When the beans are young and tender, they are delicious that way, but as they mature the pods, though still green, become very tough. Cut the pods open following directions for limas. If the shell beans are very mature, they may need to be peeled! Yes, it is a lot of work. To freeze shelled beans, blanch them for 4 to 5 minutes, chill, and freeze. Very young pods can be frozen following directions for snap beans.

Other Fresh Shell Beans

Cranberry beans, white beans and kidney beans are shelled like mature snap beans. Black-eyed peas have pods that fit snugly around each seed and they are a giant headache to shell, but worth it in the end for they are so delicious. Most of these shell beans are available frozen, also canned, alone or with other beans. They are sometimes sold already shelled. In general, cook them, or freeze them, like limas. Adjust the time for cooking to the size of the beans.

A Note to Cooks

Some of the recipes call for the use of a blender or food processor. If you lack these appliances, do not discard the recipes. Any food can be sliced, chopped or minced with a chef's knife on a chopping board. A mortar and pestle can be used for grating, and there are inexpensive hand-operated utensils for shredding. The best tool for puréeing is the hand-operated food mill, available in several sizes.

Unsalted butter and olive oil were used in testing recipes. If it matters to the recipe, the ingredient list will specify "unsalted butter"; otherwise use what you prefer, but remember to adjust salt. If butter is prohibited, use margarine instead. Any vegetable oil or polyunsaturated oil can be substituted for olive, but the taste will be slightly different.

All recipes use relatively low amounts of salt and very little sugar; if you prefer more or less, adjust to taste. If either is prohibited, simply omit. You may want to adjust flavor with a little lemon juice or an additional pinch of an herb if salt is omitted. If fructose is permitted, use that in place of cane sugar.

■ Ingredients are listed in **bold** type when they are first mentioned in the instructions and thereafter whenever it seems helpful in following the directions.

Fresh Green Peas

preparation time: 10 minutes
cooking time: 12 to 20 minutes
serves 6

2 pounds fresh green peas in pods
1 teaspoon sugar
1 teaspoon salt
butter
minced fresh parsley

1. Shell the **peas,** but save 20 perfect **pods.** Wash pods and cut off the stems. Tie pods in a large piece of cheesecloth and put in a saucepan with 3 cups **water.** Bring to a boil and simmer for 10 minutes. The pods add extra flavor.

2. Lift out and discard the bag of pods. Dissolve **sugar** and **salt** in the water, bring water again to a boil, and add the peas. Simmer until peas are tender. Start checking after 12 minutes; young peas may be tender, but larger peas may need up to 20 minutes. It is not possible to estimate the time in advance, because the tenderness depends on the season and growing conditions. Also, watch carefully, as it is easy to burn peas. Ideally, the water should be nearly all absorbed.

3. Drain off cooking liquid if there is a lot left; if not much remains, let it mix with **melted butter** to your taste. Sprinkle with **parsley**—the contrast of 2 greens is very attractive—and mix.

variations: If the peas are gathered or purchased late in the season, and are large or even beginning to sprout, double the sugar and add the salt only at the end (salt may toughen the skins, which are already a little tougher than the skins of early peas).

If you lack fresh peas, use 2 to 3 cups frozen peas (two 10-ounce packages) and only 1 cup water. Reduce cooking time to about 10 minutes, but check for doneness to be sure. Another good addition for frozen peas is a tiny pinch of fresh or dried rosemary.

9

Green Pea Soup (Potage Saint-Germain)

preparation time: 15 minutes
cooking time: about 50
minutes
serves 6

3 pounds fresh peas in pods
5 cups water
4 shallots
2 celery ribs with leaves
1/2 pound Boston lettuce, or other soft-leaf lettuce
2 ounces butter
1 teaspoon sugar
2 pinches of dried rosemary
1 white onion, 1 ounce
salt and pepper

This soup can be made in larger quantities and frozen; use 2-cup containers and defrost in the refrigerator overnight. The French name comes from a town once famous for growing peas.

1. Shell the **peas,** but save 30 perfect pods. Wash pods, cut off stems, and tie pods in a large piece of cheesecloth. Put them in a large soup kettle with the 5 cups **water.** Bring to a boil, simmer for 10 minutes, then lift out and discard the bag of pods. Keep the kettle of water.
2. Peel and mince **shallots.** Wash and dry **celery,** and cut into thin slices, including the leaves. Wash and dry **lettuce** and cut into shreds.
3. Melt **butter** in a large skillet and sauté **shallots** until translucent. Stir in **celery** and **lettuce** and cook until tender.
4. Sprinkle vegetables with the **sugar** and **rosemary** and pour in 1 cup of the liquid from the soup kettle. Bring to a boil, then transfer the whole vegetable mixture to the kettle. Add the **peas.** Bring to a boil and simmer uncovered for about 30 minutes; the peas should be very tender.
5. Before peas are quite done, use a slotted spoon to lift out about 18 cooked peas and set aside. Also peel the **white onion,** slice into rounds, and blanch them for 2 minutes. Rinse onion rounds in cold water and separate into rings. Set aside for garnish.
6. When soup is done, put everything in the kettle through a food mill (this is the best method as it removes hulls and fibers). Return the purée to the kettle, season with **salt** and **pepper** to taste, and bring to serving temperature.
7. Ladle into a tureen, or into soup bowls. Garnish with the **onion rings** and reserved **whole peas.**

Green Pea and Tomato Soup (Potage Mongole)

preparation time: 15 minutes,
plus time to make green
pea soup
cooking time: 25 minutes
serves 6 to 8

3 cups Green Pea Soup (preceding recipe)
2 pounds ripe tomatoes
2 large leeks
1 ounce butter
2 cups chicken stock
1 teaspoon salt
sugar (optional)
3 tablespoons snipped fresh chives
3 tablespoons minced parsley

1. Make the **pea soup,** or defrost it if frozen.

2. Wash **tomatoes,** remove cores, and chop. Wash **leeks,** cut off roots and about half of the green leaves, and chop the rest of the leeks. Wash the chopped leeks again, and drain well.

3. In a saucepan melt the **butter** and sauté **leeks** until translucent. Lift out about a third of the leeks, letting the butter drain off into the pan, and set aside for garnish.

4. Add **tomatoes** to leeks remaining in the pan, and cook over moderate heat, stirring often, until tomatoes are soft. Add **stock** and **salt** and simmer until tomatoes are dissolved.

5. Purée **tomato mixture** through a food mill into a bowl. Taste the purée; you may want to add a little **sugar** or more **salt.** Measure 3 cups and combine with the **green pea soup.** Mix well, and heat to serving temperature.

6. Combine the reserved **chopped leeks,** the **snipped chives** and **minced parsley.** Sprinkle the mixture on the soup in a tureen or individual bowls or, if you prefer, stir it in.

11

Curried Cream of Pea Soup

preparation time: 15 minutes,
plus time for chilling soup
cooking time: about 40
minutes
serves 6 to 8

3 pounds fresh green peas in pods
1 small yellow onion, 2 ounces
4 shallots
2 ounces butter
1-1/2 teaspoons curry powder
1/2 teaspoon whole cuminseeds, crushed
pinch of saffron
3 cups chicken stock
rind of 1 orange, in a long spiral
salt and pepper
1 cup light cream
1/2 cup plain yogurt
watercress leaves

1. Shell the **peas;** for this recipe discard the pods. Peel and mince **onion** and **shallots.** Melt **butter** in a soup kettle and sauté onion and shallots until translucent.

2. Stir in **curry powder,** the crushed **cuminseeds** and the **saffron.** Cook, stirring, until curry releases its characteristic odor and the onions begin to brown.

3. Add **peas, stock,** and **orange rind;** bring to a boil, and simmer uncovered until peas are very tender, about 30 minutes.

4. Discard **orange rind.** Put the whole soup mixture through a food mill into a bowl. Taste the purée and season generously as cold tends to flatten all seasonings. It is better to season while purée is hot so that salt dissolves and is evenly distributed.

5. Cool the **purée.** Beat **cream** and **yogurt** together and mix into the soup. Serve cool or chilled in cream-soup bowls, each bowl garnished with a few **watercress leaves.**

Green Peas à la Française

preparation time: 10 minutes
cooking time: 30 minutes
serves 6

2 pounds fresh green peas in pods
6 large lettuce leaves, or more
1/2 pound small white onions (silverskins)
1 teaspoon sugar
1 cup water
2 ounces butter
salt and pepper

1. Shell the **peas.** Wash the **lettuce leaves.** While they are still dripping, place them in a saucepan with a tight-fitting cover. Use more than 6 leaves if necessary to make a layer at least 3 leaves thick. Put the peas in the pan on top of the leaves.
2. Cut off the roots of the little **onions** but do not peel them. Cut a cross in the root end. Drop them into another saucepan and cover with boiling water. Boil for 5 minutes. Drain onions and pull off the outer layer of peel; trim root and stem ends if necessary. Quarter or chop the **onions** and add to the peas with the **sugar.**
3. Add the cup of **water,** cover saucepan, and bring to a boil. Reduce to a bare simmer and cook over low heat for 20 to 30 minutes, until peas are tender. Most of the water will be absorbed.
4. Lift out and discard the **lettuce leaves.** Add **butter** to the pan and sprinkle peas and onions with **salt** and **pepper** to taste. Toss to mix well.

variations: Fresh mint leaves or dried mint can be added for a delicious new taste.
Instead of using whole lettuce leaves to make a nest, shred the lettuce and mix it into the peas for cooking. Serve all the vegetables together.
For frozen peas, use shredded lettuce. Cook lettuce and onions together for 10 to 15 minutes before adding the peas.

Purée of Fresh Green Peas

preparation time: 10 minutes
cooking time: 20 to 30 minutes
serves 8

3 pounds fresh green peas in pods
1-1/2 teaspoons sugar
3 ounces butter
salt and pepper

Use as a vegetable accompaniment, or as a filling for tomatoes, or combine with other purées. Frozen peas are an excellent and quick substitute for this basic recipe.

1. Shell the **peas.** Cook them in water to cover with the **sugar** until they are very tender and softer than usual—20 minutes or longer.
2. Drain the **peas;** the cooking liquid can be saved for soup or stock making. Put peas through a food mill into a bowl. Beat in the **butter,** and season with **salt** and **pepper** to taste.
3. If the purée is too moist, heat it in a heavy pan set on an asbestos pad over low heat. Stir the purée with a wooden spoon or paddle to prevent burning, and heat until the texture is just right.

Clamart Garnish

Purée of Fresh Green Peas
2 egg yolks

This garnish takes its name from the village of Clamart, five miles from the Cathedral of Notre Dame in Paris, which a century ago was a market-garden area famous for peas. Today Clamart has been swallowed up by Paris.

1. Make **Purée of Fresh Green Peas** (preceding recipe), using only 2 ounces butter. Season, and dry over low heat if necessary.
2. Beat **2 egg yolks** lightly, then beat them into the purée.
3. Spoon the purée into poached artichoke bottoms to garnish a roast or a pasta or rice dish. Or fill cherry tomatoes or halves of medium-size tomatoes, and sprinkle with minced parsley. Or spoon into a pastry bag and pipe the mixture around coquilles (shell-shaped baking dishes) holding fish or shellfish mixtures, or around the edge of a plank, in the same fashion as Duchess Potatoes. For these uses, the completed coquille or planked food is usually finished in the broiler. To encourage browning, the top can be brushed with **melted butter** or **egg wash** (1 egg yolk mixed with 1 tablespoon water), but it takes only a few minutes so the rest of the food should be on the point of serving.
4. Or spoon the purée onto a large serving platter to make individual "nests" with raised edges. In each one, serve sliced and sautéed sweetbreads, garnished with glazed pearl onions, or creamed white meat of chicken with mushrooms. A beautiful presentation, and a change from Duchess Potatoes.

Peas and Carrots

preparation time: 15 minutes
cooking time: 25 minutes
serves 4 to 6

3 pounds fresh green peas in pods
1 bay leaf
salt
2 teaspoons sugar
12 ounces slender carrots
2 shallots
2 ounces butter
3 tablespoons minced parsley

What! This old cliché? Yes, this can be delicious when made with fresh vegetables, and when one remembers that the two chief ingredients need to be cooked separately.

1. Shell **peas,** cover with a large amount of water, and add the **bay leaf,** 1/2 teaspoon **salt** and 1 teaspoon **sugar.** Bring to a boil and simmer for 15 minutes, or as long as needed to have tender peas, but not overcooked. Pour off about 1/2 cup of the cooking liquid and reserve it. Drain the peas, rinse with cold water, and drain again.

2. Wash, scrape, and trim **carrots.** Cut them into crosswise rounds, or halve them and cut each half into julienne strips. Cover with water, add 1/2 teaspoon **salt** and remaining 1 teaspoon **sugar,** bring to a boil, and simmer for about 8 minutes. Carrots should be tender but not mushy (which is the main fault of restaurant carrots). Drain carrots.

3. Peel and mince **shallots.** Melt **butter** in a saucepan and sauté **shallots** until translucent. Add drained **carrots** and stir for 1 minute. Toss in the **peas.** Pour in a few tablespoons of the reserved cooking liquid, mix all together, and heat to serving temperature. Add more **salt** to taste. Use more of the cooking liquid if necessary to keep the mixture just moistened. Stir in the **parsley** and serve without reheating. This dish is good with any meat or poultry.

variation: If you can find tiny baby carrots, they can be used whole; be sure not to overcook them.

Italian Peas

preparation time: 10 minutes
cooking time: 35 minutes
serves 6

2 pounds fresh green peas in pods
12 ounces frozen pearl onions, defrosted
6 ounces prosciutto
1-1/2 ounces unsalted butter
1/2 cup chicken stock
pinch of sugar
2 tablespoons chopped Italian parsley

For this recipe buy very young pods with baby peas, or use 2 cups frozen baby peas (petits pois).

1. Shell **peas.** Pour boiling water over **onions,** let them stand for 1 minute, then drain. Chop **prosciutto.**
2. Melt **butter** in a deep skillet. Add **onions** and sauté, turning them with a wooden spoon, until they are golden. Add **prosciutto** and **peas,** mix, then pour in **stock** and add the pinch of **sugar.** As soon as stock comes to a boil, cover the skillet and simmer for 20 to 25 minutes, until peas are tender. Peas can burn, so check after 10 minutes and add a little more stock if necessary.
3. When peas are tender, the stock should be almost all absorbed. Stir in the **parsley** and serve at once.

Peas in a Hurry

preparation time: 5 minutes
cooking time: 15 to 20 minutes
serves 2 or 3

1 package (10 ounces) frozen peas
1 onion, 2 to 3 ounces
1 tablespoon vegetable oil
1 tablespoon butter
1/2 cup water
salt and pepper
pinch of garlic powder
1 teaspoon sugar (optional)

1. Remove **peas** from freezer. Peel and mince **onion.** Heat **oil** and **butter** in a saucepan and sauté **onion** until golden and just beginning to brown at the edges.
2. Add **water** and bring to a boil. Stir in **peas;** add **salt** and **pepper** to taste and **garlic powder.** Cover and cook over moderate heat for about 15 minutes.
3. Taste peas; if they lack sweetness, add the **sugar.** If the water has not evaporated, cook uncovered for a few minutes longer.

variation: Instead of garlic powder, use a pinch of your favorite herb (tarragon, marjoram, rosemary). The method can be used for fresh peas, but you will have to cook them a little longer.

Peas, Mushrooms and Pasta

preparation time: 15 minutes
cooking time: 35 to 40 minutes
serves 6

3 pounds fresh green peas in pods
1 pound fresh mushrooms
4 shallots
12 ounces pasta bowknots or tiny shells
salt
3 ounces butter
1 cup light cream
3 tablespoons snipped chives, or mixed parsley and chives

This delicious dish goes with everything. You can double or triple the recipe and serve in a huge casserole for a party.

1. Shell **peas** and cook them following the recipe for Fresh Green Peas (see Index), but do not butter them.
2. Wipe **mushrooms** with a damp cloth and trim the stems. Separate stems and caps. Chop stems, and cut caps into quarters. Peel and mince **shallots.**
3. Drop **pasta** into a large pot of boiling water with 2 teaspoons **salt** and cook for 6 to 8 minutes, according to the size of the pasta. Drain pasta.
4. Melt **butter** in a large saucepan and sauté **shallots** and **mushroom stems** for 5 minutes. Add **caps** and continue to cook until mushrooms release a lot of liquid. Pour off the liquid into a bowl and continue to cook mushrooms until lightly browned.
5. Add **peas** and **pasta,** mix well, then pour in the **cream** and the **mushroom liquid.** Cook over low heat until everything is hot and well mixed. The sauce should thicken somewhat, but do not let it boil. Sprinkle with **chives** and serve.

Venetian Rice and Peas (Risi e Bisi)

preparation time: 15 minutes
cooking time: about 40
minutes
serves 6

2 pounds fresh green peas in pods
1 onion, 3 ounces
2 tablespoons oil
2 ounces unsalted butter
4 cups chicken stock, or half stock, half water
1 cup Italian round-grain rice
1-1/2 ounces Parmesan cheese

A famous dish from Italy, it was traditionally served by the Doges of Venice at the feast for St. Mark. It should be moist, like a Mexican "dry rice soup," rather than dry like a pilaf. Excellent with poultry or veal.

1. Shell **peas;** there should be 2 to 3 cups. Peel and mince the **onion.** Heat **oil** and **butter** in a deep saucepan and sauté onion until golden and beginning to brown on the edges.
2. Pour in the **peas** and stir until they are coated with butter and oil. Pour in 1 cup of the **stock** and let it come to a boil.
3. Pour in the **rice,** stir, and cover. Leave the pot over low heat until the liquid is almost absorbed. Before the mixture becomes dry, add another cup of **stock.** When that stock is almost absorbed, add another cup of **liquid.** Finally add the last cup. After all liquid is added and the rice has cooked for about 25 minutes, both rice and peas should be tender. Add a little more **liquid** if necessary.
4. Grate the **cheese.** Remove saucepan from heat and stir in the cheese.

variation: Use 2 to 3 ounces prosciutto or cooked smoked ham, or meaty bacon. Chop or dice the meat and sauté it with the onion. If the meat is fatty, use less oil and butter. This makes an excellent vegetable main dish; serve with a green salad with tomatoes.

Indian Curried Peas and Cheese

preparation time: 15 to 20
minutes
cooking time: about 40
minutes, plus time to cool
serves 6

3 pounds fresh green peas in pods
2 onions, 3 ounces each
1 hot green chile pepper
1/4 cup light vegetable or salad oil
1-1/2 teaspoons curry powder
1 teaspoon ground turmeric
1 cup water
3 cups dry-curd low-salt cottage cheese
salt
10 fresh mint leaves

1. Shell **peas.** Peel and mince **onions.** Wearing rubber or plastic gloves, slit open the **hot pepper** and rinse off seeds. Discard stem and ribs. Halve the pepper. Mince about 4 teaspoons for the recipe (or use more to taste), and refrigerate the rest.
2. Heat the **oil** in a large saucepan and add the **onions.** Sauté until translucent. Stir in **curry powder** and **turmeric** and stir over low heat until fragrant and browned.
3. Pour in **peas,** mix, then add the cup of **water.** Cover the pan and simmer for about 20 minutes, until peas are tender. If the water evaporates too soon, add a little more, 2 tablespoons at a time.
4. Stir in **cottage cheese** and minced **chile pepper** and continue to simmer and stir until cheese is well mixed and everything is hot. Season with **salt** to taste. Set aside to cool.
5. Wash and dry **mint leaves** and sprinkle over the mixture. Serve as a cold vegetable; good with fish and poultry, or as a vegetarian main course.

variations: Before mixing in the cheese, purée the curried pea and onion mixture in a food processor or with a food mill.
Lacking good fresh peas, use 4 cups frozen peas; they need only about 10 minutes to cook.
Use butter, or butter and oil, instead of all vegetable or salad oil.

Green Pea Salad

preparation time: 20 minutes
cooking time: 20 to 25 minutes
serves 4

2 pounds fresh green peas in pods
salt
1/2 teaspoon sugar
1 onion, 3 ounces
1 teaspoon grated fresh horseradish
2 tablespoons dairy sour cream
lemon juice
1/4 pound fresh spinach
1/4 pound iceberg lettuce

1. Shell **peas.** Cook in 2 cups **water** with 1/2 teaspoon **salt** and the **sugar** until tender, 20 to 25 minutes. Drain, rinse with cold water, and drain again.
2. Peel **onion** and drop into the bowl of a food processor fitted with the steel blade. Chop until minced. Add drained **peas** and quickly purée. Mix **horseradish** and **sour cream** into the purée. Add a few drops of **lemon juice,** or to your taste, and adjust the **salt.** Let it cool.
3. Wash **spinach** thoroughly, pull off stems, and tear large leaves into 2 or 3 pieces. Chop **lettuce,** mix with spinach, and make a bed on a large salad platter or divide among 4 salad plates. Divide the cold **pea purée** among the plates.

variations: Sprinkle with minced parsley or garnish with cherry tomatoes. This is a good dish for buffet service. To make more, just multiply all the ingredients.
Use 2 cups frozen peas if you lack fresh. Use other greens for the salad base. If you do not have fresh horseradish, use prepared horseradish, but drain it well. In that case omit the lemon juice.

Tomatoes Filled with Green Pea Salad

preparation time: 30 minutes
cooking time: 20 minutes
serves 6

2 pounds fresh green peas in pods
8 scallions, no thicker than a pencil
1/2 pound perfect button mushrooms
5 ounces canned water chestnuts
6 perfect tomatoes, each 6 to 8 ounces
3 tablespoons fresh lemon juice
1 teaspoon salt
1/4 teaspoon dry mustard
1/2 cup olive oil
1/4 cup heavy cream
1 tablespoon drained capers
1 bunch of watercress
3 Belgian endives

Serve these tomatoes as a salad, or as a first course, with crisp bread or tiny biscuits.

1. Shell **peas** and cook following the recipe for Fresh Green Peas (see Index), but do not butter them.
2. Wash and trim **scallions,** and cut them into rings. Wipe **mushrooms** with a damp cloth and trim stems. Slice mushrooms. Drain **water chestnuts,** rinse with fresh water, and slice.
3. Wash **tomatoes,** cut off the tops, and scoop them out without damaging the shells. (Scooped-out portions can be used for another recipe.) Set shells upside down to drain.
4. Pour **lemon juice** into a bowl or mixer jar and dissolve **salt** and **mustard** in it. Pour in **oil** and stir or shake to mix. Pour in the **cream** and mix again; the dressing should thicken somewhat.
5. Combine **peas, scallions, mushrooms** and **water chestnuts,** and pour in **dressing.** Mix well. Divide the salad among the **tomatoes,** and garnish the tops with a few **capers.**
6. Wash and dry **watercress** and **endives.** Cut endives into rounds and cut off all the leafy watercress sprigs, discarding most of the stems. Toss both together and make a bed on each of 6 salad plates. Arrange 1 tomato on each plate.

Green Pea Soufflé

preparation time: 25 minutes
cooking time: 1-1/4 to 1-1/2
hours
serves 8

3 pounds fresh green peas in pods
salt
sugar
2 ounces unsalted butter
1 tablespoon grated hard cheese (Parmesan, Romano)
3 ounces white onions
1/2 pound mushrooms
1 teaspoon celery salt
1/4 teaspoon curry powder
3 tablespoons unbleached flour
2 cups light cream, approximately
3 ounces Munster cheese
4 egg yolks, at room temperature
6 egg whites, at room temperature

Serve as a vegetable main course, as a separate vegetable course or first course, or as an accompaniment to chicken or ham.

1. Shell **peas,** and blanch them in a large amount of boiling water with 1 teaspoon **salt** and 1 teaspoon **sugar** until very tender, 12 to 20 minutes depending on the size and maturity of the peas. (If peas are older and larger, add a little more sugar.) Drain, rinse with cold water, and drain again.
2. Purée the **peas** in a food processor, or through a food mill. There should be a generous 2 cups purée. This can be done a day ahead; cool the purée and refrigerate it.
3. Use about 1/2 ounce of the **butter** to coat the inside of a 2-quart soufflé dish. Sprinkle the butter coating with the **grated hard cheese.** Butter a double layer of foil large enough to wrap around the soufflé dish. Wrap the foil around the dish, buttered side toward the inside, and tie it in place with string.
4. Peel **onions** and mince. (If you have a food processor, use it for this step.) Trim stems of **mushrooms,** and wipe mushrooms with a damp cloth. Separate stems from caps, and chop both **stems** and **caps.**
5. Melt remaining **butter** in a large saucepan. Sauté minced **onion** and **mushroom stems** until onion is golden and tender. Add minced **mushroom caps** and sauté until mushrooms release a lot of liquid. Pour off the liquid into a 2-cup measure. Continue to sauté mushrooms until they begin to turn brown on the edges.

6. Sprinkle the vegetables with the **celery salt** and **curry powder** (do not use more than this amount of curry powder—it is a flavoring that should be barely discernible). Stir in the **flour.** Add enough **cream** to the mushroom liquid to make 2 cups and pour it into the roux. Stir to mix well and cook over low heat until the sauce is thick.

7. Stir the **purée of green peas** into the sauce and heat the mixture over low heat. Meanwhile, cut **Munster cheese** into small chunks. When the sauce mixture is very hot, remove from heat and stir in the cheese. The cheese will melt in the retained heat. Preheat oven to 350°F.

8. The **eggs** should be separated while cold. Let them rest in separate bowls while the other preparation is going on; they are easier to beat when at room temperature. Beat the **egg yolks** until well mixed. Stir in a large spoonful of the hot **sauce mixture,** then combine with the rest of the sauce. Put the saucepan of sauce in the freezer to cool for a few minutes.

9. Beat **egg whites** with a pinch of **salt** until stiff peaks stand straight up when the beater is withdrawn. Stir about a third of the egg whites into the **cooled sauce.** Then scoop the mixture into the bowl of egg whites, and with a spatula fold the two mixtures together.

10. Spoon the **soufflé batter** into the prepared dish, filling it to the top. Bake the soufflé for 45 minutes to 1 hour; it should be brown on top. The soufflé has a beautiful green color and delicate taste.

variations: When fresh peas are lacking, use frozen peas, about 20 ounces. Cook them as directed on the packages, and rinse with cold water. (With frozen peas, the green color of the soufflé is sharper, but the flavor is better with fresh peas.)

Any soft cheese can be used instead of Munster—Tilsit, Monterey Jack, etc.

Green Tart

preparation time: 30 minutes
cooking time: about 1 hour
serves 12 for first course, 6 to 8
as accompaniment

1 pound short pastry
1-1/2 ounces butter
1 pound fresh green peas in pods
salt
1/2 teaspoon sugar
1/2 pound green snap beans
1/2 pound zucchini
1/2 pound broccoli
1/2 pound fresh spinach
1 small leek
1 tablespoon olive oil
2 tablespoons unbleached flour
1-1/2 cups chicken stock
3 ounces blue cheese
chopped parsley

This tart can be made with already cooked leftover vegetables, and other combinations are possible. Other cheeses can be used.

1. Make the **pastry** (or use frozen or packaged pastry), and roll it out to a sheet about 1/8 inch thick. **Butter** a 10-inch porcelain quiche dish or other large pie dish and fit the pastry, without stretching it, into the dish. Press to the sides and trim off excess pastry. Set aside in a cool place or refrigerate.
2. Shell **peas** and blanch in boiling water with a pinch of **salt** and the **sugar** until just done. Drain, rinse with cold water, and drain again. Wash **snap beans,** top and tail them, and blanch with a pinch of **salt.** Drain and rinse like the peas. Wash and trim **zucchini** and **broccoli** and blanch and refresh these also. Finally wash **spinach** thoroughly, blanch for 2 minutes, drain, refresh, and chop. Cut zucchini and broccoli into small chunks. Combine all these vegetables in a mixing bowl. Preheat oven to 375°F.
3. Wash and chop the **leek.** Heat **oil** and remaining **butter** in a saucepan and sauté leek until translucent. Stir in the **flour,** then the **stock,** and stir over low heat until the sauce is thick and smooth.
4. Remove sauce from heat and crumble the **cheese** into it. Let the cheese melt in the retained heat of the sauce, then pour it into the **vegetables** and mix well. Spoon the filling into the chilled **pastry.**
5. Cover the tart with a sheet of foil and bake it for 15 minutes. Remove foil and bake for about 15 minutes longer, until pastry is crisp. Sprinkle with **parsley.** Serve hot or warm.

Snow Peas with Mushrooms and Gingerroot

preparation time: 10 minutes
cooking time: about 12
    minutes
serves 4

1/2 pound fresh snow peas
1/2 pound fresh mushrooms
2 ounces fresh gingerroot
3 shallots
2 tablespoons light vegetable oil
1/4 to 1/2 cup chicken stock
1 ounce medium-dry sherry

1. Wash **peas,** top and tail them, and string them. Put in a saucepan, cover with boiling water, and let them stand, not over heat, for 1 minute. Drain, rinse with cold water, and drain again.
2. Cut stem ends of **mushrooms,** wipe with a damp cloth, and cut through cap and stem into thin slices. Peel and mince **gingerroot** and **shallots.**
3. Heat **oil** in a skillet and sauté **gingerroot** for about 1 minute. With a slotted spoon transfer it to a plate. Put **shallots** in the skillet and sauté until golden. Add **mushrooms** and sauté until they release their liquid.
4. Add blanched **snow peas,** return the **gingerroot,** and pour in 1/4 cup **chicken stock.** Bring to a boil and simmer for about 3 minutes, until peas are cooked but still crunchy. Add more of the stock if necessary, but mixture should be moist, not soupy.
5. Pour in **sherry,** heat, and serve to accompany any poultry or shellfish. Rice is a logical companion.

variations: Frozen snow peas and canned sliced mushrooms can be used in an emergency. Do not blanch the peas. Use the mushroom liquid in place of chicken stock and sauté mushrooms for only 1 minute.
For a delicious variation use canned Chinese straw mushrooms, drained.

27

Poached Duck with Snow Peas and Onions

preparation time: 30 minutes
cooking time: about 3 hours for
duck and stock; about 30
minutes for completion
serves 6

2 ducks, about 5 pounds each
salt
1 large bay leaf
1 large celery rib with leaves
1 large onion, stuck with 2 cloves
1 large carrot, scraped and slivered
1 pound snow peas
1 pound very small white onions (silverskins)
    or frozen pearl onions
1 shallot
1 hard-cooked egg, shelled
3 tablespoons chopped parsley
1 ounce butter
6 small bread rectangles, toasted
1-1/2 ounces sweet Madeira
1 tablespoon beurre manié (butter and flour mixed together)

This is a party dish, somewhat fussy to prepare, but no step is difficult. Start a day ahead. Only the breast meat and livers are used in this recipe, but the rest of the birds contribute to the flavor of the stock and can be used for a salad on another occasion.

1. Have the **ducks** quartered. Rinse and trim any giblets, but separate the **livers** and tie them in a piece of cheesecloth. Place all duck pieces except livers in a large heavy kettle or roaster, cover with room-temperature water, and bring to a simmer. Add 1 tablespoon **salt,** the **bay leaf,** the **celery,** the **large onion** and the **carrot.** Poach the **ducks** until the breast meat is just tender, about 45 minutes.
2. Remove breast quarters from the kettle. Separate wings and skin and carefully bone the **breast meat** completely. Cover breast meat when cool, and refrigerate. Meanwhile return wings, skin and bones to the kettle and add the **duck livers.** Continue to cook for about 20 minutes longer, until legs are tender.
3. Remove all the **duck pieces** and **giblets.** When cool enough to handle, bone **duck** and return bones and skin to the kettle. Cool remaining duck portions and refrigerate. Also refrigerate the **livers.** Bring the poaching liquid again to a simmer and cook for about 2 hours longer, until you have a flavorful **stock.**

4. Pour **stock** through a colander to discard bones, then through a fine sieve lined with cheesecloth. Cool the stock, then refrigerate. Remove the fat, which will rise to the top. Measure 4 cups **stock** and reduce to 2 cups. Reserve the rest for Steps 5 and 6.

5. Next day, wash **snow peas,** top and tail them, and string them. Blanch them for 1 minute, drain, rinse with cold water, and drain again. Cut a cross in the root end of each unpeeled **onion,** cover them with some unreduced **duck stock,** and bring to a boil. Simmer for 10 minutes, then drain and cool. Peel **onions.** (If you are using frozen onions, cover them with stock and simmer until defrosted.)

6. Peel the **shallot** and drop into the bowl of a food processor fitted with the steel blade. Add the **hard-cooked egg,** the **duck livers, parsley** and **butter,** with **salt** to taste, and process to a small pâté. Add a few teaspoons of duck stock if necessary to get the right texture. Spread **pâté** on the **toast rectangles;** they will be used for garnish.

7. Cut **duck breasts** into long slivers. Pour the reduced 2 cups **duck stock** into a large saucepan, bring to a simmer, then add peeled **onions** and simmer until tender. Add **duck pieces,** heat, then add **snow peas** and heat for about 2 minutes. With a skimmer transfer the duck and vegetables to a serving platter and keep warm.

8. Add **Madeira** to the **stock** and boil rapidly for 2 minutes. Adjust **salt** to taste. Then add the mixture of **butter** and **flour** (beurre manié) in tiny crumbles to the stock until it is somewhat thickened, not pasty. Spoon a little over the duck; serve the rest separately. Garnish the platter with the **toast pieces.** Serve with a brown rice pilaf and a salad of greens with orange sections and black olives.

Snow Pea Salad

preparation time: 10 to 15 minutes
cooking time: 5 minutes
serves 4

1 pound fresh snow peas
8 scallions, as thick as a pencil
4 tender celery ribs
4 to 6 plum tomatoes
1/2 teaspoon salt
1/2 teaspoon sugar
2 tablespoons fresh lemon juice
1 teaspoon prepared mustard
4 to 6 tablespoons olive oil
shredded lettuce (optional)
black pepper

1. Wash **snow peas,** top and tail them, and string them. Blanch them for 3 minutes; they should still be crisp. Drain, rinse with cold water, drain again, and roll in a towel to dry.
2. Wash and trim **scallions.** Cut off all but 1 inch of the green part, and cut the rest at an angle into 2-inch slivers. Wash and dry **celery ribs** and cut at an angle into 2-inch sections. Blanch and peel **tomatoes,** and cut from stem to blossom end into thin wedges.
3. Toss all the **vegetables** together. In a small mixing bowl, stir **salt** and **sugar** into **lemon juice** until dissolved. With a whisk beat in the **mustard** and **oil** until well mixed. Taste, you may want more **salt.** Pour over vegetables and toss.
4. Serve plain or on a bed of **lettuce,** and sprinkle with freshly ground **black pepper.**

variations: Changing the lemon juice to white-wine vinegar and olive oil to walnut oil will give a different taste. Use fewer scallions, or substitute chives. Omit mustard from the dressing if you like.

Buttered Snap Beans

preparation time: 10 minutes
cooking time: 10 minutes
serves 4

1 pound green or yellow snap beans
1/2 teaspoon salt
1-1/2 ounces butter
2 tablespoons minced parsley

Choose very small crisp beans, whether green or yellow. (It is not easy to find tiny beans, but it is worthwhile looking for them.)

1. Wash **beans,** top and tail them, and cover them with several quarts of water in a large saucepan. Add the **salt.** Bring to a boil and boil for 8 to 10 minutes, until beans are done to your taste. Lift out a bean and taste it to be sure. If you overcook them by so little as 2 minutes, they will lose color and texture.

2. Drain **beans,** rinse with cold water or plunge into a bowl of ice water, and drain again. This can be done well in advance of serving.

3. When ready to finish your meal preparations, melt **butter** in a saucepan and toss the **beans** in it until they are all coated with butter and hot. Sprinkle with **parsley** and serve.

variations: An old cliché, but delicious nevertheless: Increase butter to 2-1/2 ounces and in it sauté 1/4 cup slivered blanched almonds until golden. Add beans, toss to heat well and mix, and serve. Use parsley or not, as you please.

When melting butter in Step 3, add several pinches of your favorite herb—rosemary, tarragon, chervil—and toss with the blanched beans.

Follow a German custom and add a large pinch of dried summer savory, or several fresh sprigs, when blanching the beans. (Savory is called "bean herb" in Germany.)

Green Soup with Legumes

preparation time: about 30
minutes
cooking time: about 50
minutes
serves 8

1 pound yellow onions
1 pound leeks
1 pound zucchini
1 pound fresh green peas in pods
1 pound green snap beans
1/2 pound fresh shell beans (cranberry beans or black-eyed peas)
1 pound fresh spinach
3 tablespoons vegetable oil
8 cups water or stock
1 bay leaf
4 fresh basil leaves, or large pinch of dried basil
salt and pepper
chopped parsley
snipped chives
grated Parmesan or Romano cheese

1. Peel and mince **onions.** Trim and wash **leeks;** retain all the green leaves. Cut leeks across into thin slices, wash them again, and drain well. Wash, scrape, and trim **zucchini,** and cut into 1/2-inch cubes. Shell the **peas;** wash and trim **green beans;** rinse **shell beans.**

2. Wash and trim **spinach,** put in a large saucepan, and cover with boiling water. Boil for 1 minute, then drain, rinse with cold water, and drain again. Chop the **spinach.**

3. Heat the **oil** in a large soup kettle and sauté **onions** and **leeks** until translucent. Add **shell beans** and **water** or **stock, bay leaf** and **basil.** Bring to a boil and simmer for 20 minutes.

4. Cut green **snap beans** into 3 pieces each and add to the kettle, along with the fresh **peas.** Continue to simmer for 15 minutes longer.

5. Add **zucchini** and **spinach** and cook for about 5 minutes longer, until all vegetables are tender. Taste, and add **salt** and **pepper** as needed.

6. Sprinkle the soup with **parsley** and **chives** to taste. Accompany with a bowl of **grated cheese** and toast made of pita bread. This soup is thick, delicious and nutritious.

Cream of Green Bean Soup (Crème Favorite)

preparation time: 15 minutes
cooking time: about 40
minutes
serves 6 to 8

1-1/2 pounds green snap beans
salt
3 shallots
2 small celery ribs with leaves
1 tablespoon vegetable oil
1 ounce butter
6 cups chicken stock
2 egg yolks
1-1/2 cups light cream

1. Wash **beans,** top and tail them, and blanch them in boiling water with 1/2 teaspoon **salt** for about 5 minutes. Drain, rinse with cold water, and drain again. Chop the **beans** with a chef's knife, or in a food processor fitted with the steel blade.

2. Peel and mince **shallots.** Wash and dry **celery ribs** and cut into thin slices including the leaves. Heat **oil** and **butter** in a soup kettle and sauté **shallots** and **celery** until shallots are translucent.

3. Add chopped **beans** and **stock,** bring to a boil, and simmer until all the vegetables are very soft, about 30 minutes.

4. Beat **egg yolks** and **cream** together, stir a ladle of the hot soup into the mixture, and combine with the rest of the soup. Heat soup to serving temperature, stirring, but do not let it boil. Season with more **salt** if needed. If you like, garnish with a few toasted croutons.

variation: We like this cream soup with the vegetable pieces still in it, for an interesting texture. For a smooth version, purée the finished soup in a blender or food processor or push through a food mill. Reheat to serving temperature.

33

Frenched Snap Beans

preparation time: 15 minutes
cooking time: 15 minutes
serves 4

1 pound green snap beans
1/2 teaspoon salt
1 teaspoon minced fines herbes (chervil, tarragon, parsley, thyme)
1 cup water
1 ounce butter
2 tablespoons snipped fresh chives

For this recipe use larger beans, about 1/2 inch wide, but avoid those with well-developed seeds.

1. Wash **beans** and top and tail them. With a sharp knife slice beans lengthwise into 2 or 3 thin slivers; or do this in a bean slicer, which will make even slivers. (This is Frenching.)
2. Put **beans** in a heavy saucepan with a tight-fitting lid. Add **salt, fines herbes** and **water.** Bring to a boil, cover, reduce heat to a simmer, and cook for about 15 minutes, or until beans are done to your taste. Most of the water will be absorbed.
3. Drop **butter** and **chives** into the **beans** and cover the saucepan until butter is melted. Shake to mix well and serve at once.

note: Frozen Frenched beans are generally available, but they often dry out in the freezing process. Nevertheless, this recipe can be adapted to frozen beans and will make them more tasty.

Southern-Style Green Beans or Peas

preparation time: 15 minutes
cooking time: 1 to 3 hours
serves 6

1-1/2 pounds green snap beans (older, fatter beans)
    or 3 pounds fresh green peas in pods (older, fatter peas)
4 ounces salt pork, or 1 smoked ham hock
2 quarts water
sugar (optional)
salt and pepper

This may not be everyone's favorite way of preparing beans and peas, but for some it is the best of all methods.

1. Wash **beans,** top and tail them, and string them if necessary. Or shell the **peas.**
2. Put **salt pork** or **ham hock** in a large kettle, cover with water, and bring to a boil. Simmer the pork for 10 minutes. Drain.
3. Rinse out the kettle, then return **pork** to the kettle and pour in the **2 quarts water.** Bring again to a boil, cover, and simmer for 20 minutes.
4. Add **beans** or **peas,** bring again to a boil, and simmer covered for 1 hour. (Some cooks continue until vegetables have cooked for up to 3 hours; do what suits you best.) If the vegetables are mature, add 1-1/2 teaspoons **sugar,** or as much as you like, to bring out the flavor.
5. Season the cooked vegetables with **salt** and **pepper** to taste. Do not serve the pork, but spoon a few tablespoons of the **cooking liquid** over the vegetables, which will have a thin coating of fat. In this method the vegetables are no longer green.

Green Beans with Hazelnut Sauce

preparation time: 15 minutes
cooking time: 15 minutes
serves 6

1-1/2 pounds green snap beans
salt
3 ounces shelled hazelnuts
1 onion, 3 ounces
2 tablespoons olive or hazelnut oil
1/2 cup chicken stock
3/4 cup dairy sour cream
6 slices of cracked-wheat or whole-wheat bread, toasted

1. Wash **beans,** top and tail them, and blanch them in boiling water with 1/2 teaspoon **salt** for about 8 minutes. Drain, rinse with cold water, drain again; this can be done a day in advance.

2. Chop or grind **nuts;** use a food processor fitted with the steel blade for best results. Scrape nuts onto a plate. Chop the **onion.** Heat **oil** in a skillet and sauté onion until the pan begins to look dry.

3. Stir in **hazelnuts** and sauté for 1 minute. Pour in 3 tablespoons **chicken stock** and cook until stock is absorbed. Scrape the mixture into the processor and add **sour cream.** Process until you have a thick creamy sauce. Scrape sauce into a saucepan and keep warm over hot water.

4. Reheat **green beans** in remaining **chicken stock** until they are steaming Arrange 1 piece of **toast** on each of 6 salad or luncheon plates, and divide beans among the toasts. Spoon **hazelnut sauce** over the beans and serve at once, as a separate course, or to accompany poultry or veal.

variations: The sauce can be used with any fresh beans, even shell beans, but is prettiest with green beans. A walnut sauce can be made the same way; for that use walnut oil.

Omit toast and serve beans and sauce at room temperature or cold. Hazelnuts can be peeled if you like. Put them in a single layer on an ungreased baking sheet, and slide it into a preheated 350°F. oven. After 15 minutes the skins will crack. Rub the nuts, a few at a time, in a clean coarse towel; most of the skin will come off and any bits that remain are unimportant.

Sweet-and-Sour Wax Beans

preparation time: 15 minutes
cooking time: about 20
minutes
serves 6

1-1/2 pounds wax beans (yellow snap beans)
salt
1 white onion, 1 ounce
1 ounce fresh gingerroot
1 ounce butter
1 tablespoon cornstarch
3 tablespoons sugar
1/4 cup cider vinegar
1/4 cup pineapple juice

This procedure can be used for green snap beans also. Good with pork.

1. Wash **beans,** top and tail them, and blanch them with 1/2 teaspoon **salt** for 10 minutes, or until tender. Pour off the cooking liquid and reserve it; some is needed for the recipe. Rinse beans with cold water and drain again.
2. Peel and grate both **onion** and **gingerroot.** Melt **butter** in a large saucepan and sauté onion and gingerroot until golden. Pour in 1/2 cup of the reserved **cooking liquid** and bring to a simmer.
3. In a bowl mix **cornstarch** and **sugar** and stir in **vinegar** and **pineapple juice.** Pour the mixture into the simmering liquid, stirring all the while. The sauce will thicken and start to clarify almost at once.
4. Add drained **beans** to the sauce and gently stir to coat them all with the sauce. If it seems to be too thick, add more of the bean **cooking liquid,** a few tablespoons at a time. The sauce should not be stiff or pasty, but should provide a glistening coating for the beans.

variation: Add a few tablespoons of crushed pineapple to the sauce. Garnish with diamonds of blanched red bell pepper.

Three-Bean Salad

preparation time: 30 minutes,
plus 8 hours for marinating
cooking time: 30 minutes
serves 8 to 12

1 pound shelled fresh cranberry beans
1 pound green snap beans
1 pound yellow snap beans (wax beans)
1/4 cup white-wine vinegar
2 tablespoons sugar
salt
1/2 teaspoon ground coriander
1 cup olive oil
1/2 pound plum tomatoes
1/2 pound Italian peppers
1 red onion, 4 to 6 ounces
shredded escarole or romaine (optional)

1. Pick over **cranberry beans** and remove any bits of pod. Wash **green** and **yellow beans** and top and tail them.

2. Make the dressing: Pour **vinegar** into a bowl or shaker jar and dissolve the **sugar,** 1 teaspoon **salt** and the **coriander** in it. Add **olive oil** and stir or shake to mix.

3. Cook **cranberry beans** (see Simmered Fresh Shell Beans), drain them, and while beans are still hot pour the **dressing** over them.

4. Blanch **green** and **yellow beans,** separately, in ample water, each with 1/2 teaspoon **salt,** for 8 to 10 minutes; they should still be crunchy. Drain, rinse with cold water, and drain again. Spread **beans** out on a board and cut them into pieces 1-1/2 inches long.

5. Add **snap beans** to the **cranberry beans** and mix well to combine with the dressing. Cover beans and marinate for 8 hours or overnight.

6. Blanch and peel **tomatoes** and cut into small dice. Wash **peppers,** discard stems, ribs and seeds, and cut peppers into 1-inch pieces. Peel **onion** and slice; separate slices into rings.

7. Pour off excess dressing from beans. Add the other **vegetables** to the **beans** and toss to mix everything well. Spoon onto a bed of shredded **escarole** or **romaine,** or serve without greens.

variations: The onion can be marinated with the beans; it will be milder in taste, but less crisp.
Parsley or other herbs may be added. A peeled garlic clove can be dropped into the marinating beans, to be removed later.

Green Bean and Red Pepper Salad

preparation time: 15 minutes
cooking time: 8 minutes
serves 4 to 6

1 pound green snap beans, about 1/4 inch wide
pinch of dried savory
1 red bell pepper, 6 to 8 ounces
4 ounces Bermuda onion (about 1/2 onion)
1/2 teaspoon salt
2 tablespoons white-wine vinegar
1/4 cup olive oil
3 tablespoons minced fresh parsley

1. Wash and trim the **beans;** leave them whole. Drop them into a large pot of boiling water. Add the **savory.** Boil the beans for 6 to 8 minutes, until tender but still a little crunchy. Drain, rinse with cold water, and drain again.
2. Wash the **red pepper;** with a vegetable peeler remove the skin. (Or cut into quarters and broil, skin side toward the heat source, until charred. Then peel off the skin.) Discard stem, ribs and seeds. Cut **pepper** into thin slivers, about as wide as the beans.
3. Peel the **onion** and cut from top to bottom into thin slivers. Dissolve the **salt** in the **vinegar.**
4. Combine **beans, pepper slivers** and **onion slivers** in a salad bowl. Pour in the **oil** and mix gently to coat all vegetables. Pour in **vinegar,** mix again, and sprinkle with **parsley.**
5. Serve as a vegetable with cold meats or aspic dishes, or as a salad on a bed of shredded lettuce (iceberg, romaine, red-leaf).

Green Bean and Zucchini Salad

preparation time: 15 minutes
cooking time: 12 minutes
serves 6

1 pound tender young green snap beans
salt
1 pound tiny zucchini, each only 2 to 3 ounces
1 red bell pepper
1 teaspoon dried tarragon
1/2 teaspoon dried rosemary
2 tablespoons dry white wine
5 teaspoons prepared Dijon mustard
1/4 cup olive oil

1. Wash **beans,** top and tail them, and drop them into a large pot of cold water with 1/2 teaspoon **salt.** Bring to a boil and blanch them for 8 to 10 minutes, until cooked but still green and somewhat crisp. Drain, rinse with cold water until completely cold (or drop into a pan of ice water), and drain again.

2. Scrape **zucchini** unless they are fresh from the garden, trim them, and cut lengthwise into 4 to 6 pieces, depending on how fat they are. Drop them into a pot of cold water, add 1/2 teaspoon **salt,** bring to a boil and blanch for about 2 minutes, until barely cooked. Drain, rinse with cold water, and drain again.

3. Peel the **red pepper** and cut off 6 thick strips. Use the rest of the pepper for another recipe. Mix **herbs** and **white wine** in a small bowl and let the mixture stand until herbs are revived. Then stir in **mustard** and beat in the **oil.**

4. Gently mix the **vegetables** and arrange them in bundles on a salad platter or individual plates. Drape a **pepper strip** over each one, and spoon about 1 tablespoon of the **mustard dressing** over each bundle. Serve as a cold vegetable or as a salad.

variations: Adjust the balance of the dressing to your taste. If you grow your own herbs, experiment. I have sometimes made this with lemon balm instead of rosemary.

Russian Salad

preparation time: 20 minutes,
plus 1 hour for marinating
cooking time: 20 minutes, if all
vegetables are cooked at
the same time
serves 4, more as a garnish

1 pound fresh green peas in pods
1/2 pound green snap beans
1/2 pound fresh shell beans (lima beans, cranberry beans, white beans)
1/4 pound carrots
1/4 pound parsnips
salt
1/4 cup cider vinegar
1/4 teaspoon dry mustard
black pepper
1 cup salad oil
1/2 to 1 cup mayonnaise

This salad can be served by itself, but it is more usual to serve it as a garnish or as a base for other ingredients—fish, shellfish, meats.

1. Shell the **peas.** Wash **snap beans** and top and tail them. Pick over **shell beans** and remove any bits of pod. Scrape and trim **carrots** and **parsnips,** and cut both into julienne slivers.
2. Blanch each vegetable separately with a pinch of **salt;** allow 15 minutes for the **peas,** 10 minutes for **snap beans,** 15 to 20 minutes for **shell beans,** and about 10 minutes for the julienne of **carrots** and **parsnips.** Adjust all these times to the vegetables you have; they should be tender but not mushy. Drain vegetables, rinse with cold water, and drain again. Pat dry. Put all the vegetables in a large bowl and gently mix.
3. Make salad dressing: Pour **vinegar** into a mixer jar and and in it dissolve the **mustard** and 1 teaspoon **salt.** Add freshly ground **pepper** to taste. Pour in **oil** and shake well. Pour the dressing over the vegetables, toss well, and set them aside to marinate for about 1 hour. If the dressing does not cover the vegetables, turn them over now and then.
4. Drain **vegetables** (the dressing can be used for another salad). Spoon in as much **mayonnaise** as needed to hold the vegetable mixture together. Serve in Boston lettuce leaves, or in cucumber boats, or in hollowed-out tomatoes. Or mound the whole salad on a round serving platter and surround it with fish, shellfish or meat, in pieces or slices of serving size, or with halved hard-cooked eggs.

variations: Mix in chopped fresh herbs, or spinkle them over the salad. Chopped anchovy fillets or capers can be added for more pungency.

41

Salade Niçoise

preparation time: 20 minutes
cooking time: 30 minutes
serves 6 to 8

1-1/2 pounds green snap beans
salt
1 pound tiny red-skinned new potatoes
3 hard-cooked eggs
6 ripe plum tomatoes
6 anchovy fillets
2 cans (6-1/2 ounces each) oil-packed tuna fish
2 tablespoons white-wine vinegar
black pepper
1 garlic clove
6 tablespoons olive oil
12 oil-cured black olives

In Provence this salad is always served as an hors-d'oeuvre, but as you can see it is substantial enough to make a main course for lunch or supper.

1. Wash **beans,** top and tail them, and blanch them in a large amount of boiling water with 1 teaspoon **salt** for 8 to 10 minutes. Drain, rinse with cold water, and drain again.
2. Wash **potatoes** and steam them for about 20 minutes, until tender but not mushy. Peel potatoes and cut into wedges.
3. Shell the **eggs** and cut each lengthwise into 4 pieces. Blanch **tomatoes** and cut them lengthwise into halves. Blot some of the oil from **anchovies** and cut each fillet into halves. Open **tuna** and divide into 1-inch chunks. Any excess oil from tuna and anchovies can be saved for other recipes.
4. Make the dressing: Spoon **vinegar** into a mixing bowl and add **salt** and **black pepper** to taste; remember that anchovies and tuna will be salty. Peel **garlic** and push through a press into the vinegar. Pour in **oil** and beat with a whisk.
5. Use a large round or oval salad bowl, shallow rather than deep. Gently combine **green beans, potato wedges** and **tuna chunks,** and pour in half of the **dressing.** Toss to mix well, then arrange these ingredients in the center of the salad bowl. Around the edge place alternately **tomato halves** and **egg quarters.** Garnish each tomato half with an **olive,** each egg quarter with an **anchovy piece.** Sprinkle the rest of the dressing over everything.

Green Beans with Tuna (Fagiolini col Tonno)

preparation time: 15 minutes
cooking time: about 10
minutes
serves 4 to 6 as antipasto, 2 or
3 for main course

1 pound green snap beans
salt
1/4 cup olive oil
2 tablespoons lemon juice
black pepper
4 ripe plum tomatoes
1 can (6-1/2 ounces) oil-packed tuna fish

This simple but delicious dish is served as an antipasto in Italy, usually with a few other dishes. However, like Salade Niçoise it can make an excellent main course for lunch.

1. Wash **beans,** top and tail them, and blanch them in a large amount of water with 1/2 teaspoon **salt** for 8 to 10 minutes. Drain them, but do not rinse with cold water. Put the still hot beans in a bowl and pour in the **oil.** Mix gently to coat beans with oil, then add **lemon juice, black pepper** from the mill, and **salt** to taste.
2. Blanch and peel **tomatoes.** Cut them into 1/4-inch dice, discarding as many seeds as possible. Open **tuna** and divide into 1-inch chunks.
3. Arrange the **dressed beans** in a shallow serving bowl, place tuna pieces on top, and scatter **tomato dice** over all. Serve at room temperature, or warm.

variations: Instead of green beans, use fresh shell beans, if possible white beans, but any fresh beans can be used. Be sure to add oil to the cooked beans while they are still warm.
This dish can be decorated with salad greens if you like. Arugula with its pungent flavor is particularly good, but watercress makes a good substitute.

43

Italian Green-Bean Pudding (Sformato di Fagiolini)

preparation time: 20 minutes
cooking time: about 1-1/2
hours
serves 4 to 6

1 pound green snap beans
salt
3 ounces Parmesan cheese
2 ounces prosciutto
2 ounces shallots
1 ounce butter
2 tablespoons flour
3/4 cup milk
3 large eggs
1/2 teaspoon celery salt
black pepper

The baked pudding should be firm enough to be unmolded but, if it is still soft, it can be served from the dish. The pale green color with specks of rosy ham is as beautiful to look at as it is delicious. A food processor gives best results.

1. Wash **beans,** top and tail them, and blanch them in a large amount of water with 1/2 teaspoon **salt** for about 12 minutes; they should be much softer than the usual blanched beans.
2. While beans are being blanched, grate the **cheese** in a food processor fitted with the steel blade; set it aside. Chop **prosciutto** in the processor and set aside. Peel **shallots** and mince them in the processor.
3. Drain **beans,** rinse with cold water, and drain again. Cut beans into pieces and chop in the processor until they are almost puréed.
4. Use some of the **butter** to coat a 6-cup soufflé dish or pudding mold. Sprinkle a little **grated cheese** over the butter. Preheat oven to 375°F.
5. Melt remaining **butter** in a saucepan and in it sauté **shallots** until translucent. Add **prosciutto** and sauté until crisp on the edges. Stir in **flour,** then the **milk,** and cook over low heat until sauce is very thick.
6. Stir **puréed beans** into the sauce, then mix in the **cheese** until melted. Remove saucepan from heat. Beat the **eggs,** warm them with a few spoonfuls of the beans, and then mix eggs into the rest of the ingredients. Add **celery salt,** a few grinds of **black pepper,** and a little more **salt** if needed.
7. Spoon pudding into the prepared dish, set it in a basin of hot water, and slide into the oven. Cover loosely with a sheet of foil. Bake for 1 hour to 1-1/4 hours, until pudding tests done. Turn out onto a deep round plate, or serve from the dish.

Green Beans au Gratin

preparation time: 15 minutes
cooking time: about 40
minutes
serves 8

2 pounds green snap beans
salt
6 scallions
2 ounces butter
1/2 teaspoon dry mustard
1/2 teaspoon curry powder
3 tablespoons unbleached flour
1 cup chicken stock
1 cup light cream
3 ounces ground walnuts
3 ounces crumbled blue cheese
1/2 cup soft fresh bread crumbs

This is an excellent vegetable dish for a buffet meal.

1. Wash **beans,** top and tail them, and blanch them in ample water with about 1 teaspoon **salt.** Drain beans, rinse with cold water, and drain again.
2. Wash and trim **scallions;** use some of the green part, save the rest for soups. Chop scallions.
3. Melt 1 ounce of the **butter** in a large saucepan and sauté **scallions** until golden and tender. Stir in **mustard** and **curry powder,** and continue to sauté, stirring, for 2 minutes. Remove pan from heat and stir in the **flour.**
4. Return saucepan to low heat and pour in **stock** and **cream.** Cook the sauce, stirring until it is thick and smooth. Taste the sauce; you may want to add a little **salt,** but remember that the cheese is salty. Add the **beans** and mix gently to distribute beans evenly in the sauce. Transfer the whole mixture to an 8-cup shallow casserole (a lasagne dish is a good choice). Preheat oven to 350°F.
5. Combine **walnuts, cheese** and **bread crumbs,** and sprinkle evenly over the bean mixture. Bake in the oven for about 20 minutes, until casserole is bubbling around the edges, cheese is melted, and crumbs are golden.

variations: Instead of blue cheese and ground walnuts, use Cheddar cheese and slivered blanched almonds. Instead of mustard and curry powder, use Worcestershire sauce or garlic or a mixture of herbs.

Scalloped Green and Yellow Beans

preparation time: 20 minutes
cooking time: 45 minutes
serves 8

1 pound green snap beans
1 pound yellow snap beans (wax beans)
salt
6 hard-cooked eggs
2-1/2 ounces butter
2 tablespoons unbleached flour
1/4 teaspoon grated nutmeg
2 cups milk
4 ounces mixed Gruyère and Parmesan cheese, grated
1 cup soft fresh bread crumbs

This is a fancied-up version of an old-fashioned English dish. It is excellent for fast days, for vegetarian meals, or for buffet service.

1. Wash both **beans,** keeping them separate throughout. Top and tail them, and blanch them in large amounts of water, adding 1/2 teaspoon **salt** to each saucepan. Cook beans for 8 minutes only; they should still be rather crisp. Drain, rinse with cold water, and drain again.
2. Shell the **eggs** and cut across into thin slices. Use 1/2 ounce of the **butter** to coat a deep rectangular 2-quart casserole.
3. Melt 1 ounce of the **butter** in a saucepan and stir in **flour** and **nutmeg.** Pour in the **milk** and cook over low heat, stirring, until sauce is smooth and somewhat thickened. Stir in 1 ounce of the mixed **cheeses** and stir to combine. Preheat oven to 350°F.
4. Layer half of the **green beans** in the buttered casserole, then one third of the **egg slices.** Next add half of the **yellow beans** and another third of the **eggs.** Add the rest of the **green beans,** the rest of the **eggs,** finally the rest of the **yellow beans.** Pour the **sauce** into the mixture, lifting the layers if necessary to let the sauce seep through the layers.
5. Combine the rest of the mixed **cheeses** and the **crumbs** and spread in an even layer over the casserole. Cut remaining ounce of **butter** into tiny dots and drop them over the top. Bake the casserole for 30 minutes, until the topping is golden and the sauce bubbling around the edges.

Green Bean and Mushroom Casserole

preparation time: 20 minutes
cooking time: about 50
minutes, plus 20 minutes
to prepare onions
serves 6

1-1/2 pounds green snap beans
salt
12 ounces fresh mushrooms
3-1/2 ounces butter
3 tablespoons unbleached flour
1-1/2 cups light cream
white pepper
1/4 cup minced fresh parsley
2 cups French-fried onion rings

If you are preparing this casserole "from scratch," first fry the onion rings, drain them well, and set aside at room temperature.

1. Wash **beans,** top and tail them, and blanch in a large amount of water with 1/2 teaspoon **salt** for about 8 minutes; beans should still be crisp. Drain, rinse with cold water, and drain again. Turn beans into a mixing bowl.
2. Trim the stems of the **mushrooms.** Wipe mushrooms with a damp cloth; wash them only if very soiled. Separate the stems and chop them; slice the caps. Melt 1-1/2 ounces of the **butter** in a saucepan and sauté the **chopped stems** for 2 minutes. Add the **sliced caps** and sauté until mushrooms release a lot of liquid. Pour off the liquid into a bowl, and continue to cook mushrooms until browned. Add mushrooms and any remaining butter to the bowl of beans. Preheat oven to 350°F.
3. Use a little of the **butter** to coat a 6-cup casserole. Melt the remainder in the saucepan used for the mushrooms. Stir in the **flour,** then the **cream** and the reserved **mushroom liquid.** Cook the sauce over low heat, stirring often, until it is thick and smooth. Taste, and add **salt** if needed and a little **white pepper.** Stir in the **parsley,** and pour the sauce into the bowl of beans and mushrooms.
4. Gently mix the ingredients together, and spoon them into the buttered casserole. Arrange the fried **onion rings** in a rather thick layer over the top. Bake the casserole for about 30 minutes, until sauce is bubbling and onions are crisp.

variations: This dish can be made with frozen beans, canned cream of mushroom soup and packaged French-fried onions; it's good that way, but much more delicious made from scratch.
If you want a more flavorful cream sauce, add herbs or spices to taste, or cook a few shallots in the butter before adding the flour.

Beef Stew with Green Beans

preparation time: 20 minutes
cooking time: about 2 hours
serves 4 to 6

1-1/2 pounds pieces of boneless beef chuck
1/2 pound yellow onions
2 tablespoons olive oil
1 cup dry red wine
2 cups beef stock
2 cups stewed tomatoes
salt
2 large bay leaves
4 ounces celery ribs with leaves
1 large green pepper
1-1/2 pounds green snap beans

1. Rinse the pieces of **beef,** pat them dry, and cut into 1-1/2 inch pieces. Peel and chop the **onions.**
2. Heat **oil** in a skillet and sauté **onions** until they are translucent and just beginning to brown. Use a slotted spoon to transfer onions to a 3-quart kettle; leave any oil in the skillet.
3. Sauté the chunks of **beef** until they release any fat and are brown on all sides. Transfer beef to the kettle and pour in **wine, stock** and **tomatoes.** Add 1 teaspoon **salt** and the **bay leaves.** Bring to a simmer, partly cover the kettle, and cook for 1 hour.
4. Wash **celery** and pat dry. Use a swivel vegetable peeler to remove strings. Cut celery into small pieces. Wash and trim **green pepper;** discard stem, ribs and seeds, and cut pepper into small pieces. At the end of the hour, stir celery and green pepper into the stew and simmer for another hour.
5. Wash **green beans,** top and tail them, and blanch them for about 10 minutes; they should still be crisp. Rinse with cold water and drain well.
6. Test the **beef;** when tender, stir in the **beans,** mix well, and reheat the stew to serving temperature. Onions, celery, green pepper and tomatoes will be reduced to a thick flavorful purée. Serve the stew with pasta shells or bowknots.

Bean Stew with Lamb and Potatoes (Bohneneintopf)

preparation time: 15 minutes
cooking time: 1 to 1-1/2 hours
serves 4

1-1/2 pounds shoulder of lamb
1 pound fresh snap beans or very tender young broad beans
1 pound small potatoes
3 to 4 cups water
1-1/2 teaspoons salt
1/2 teaspoon summer savory
2 tablespoons flour
chopped parsley

This is a German recipe, simple but delicious home fare. Augment it with other ingredients and additional seasonings if you like.

1. Cut **lamb** into 1-inch cubes and trim off all fat. (Or have your butcher do this.) Any bones can be added to the stew pot for flavor. There should be about 1 pound fat-free boneless meat.
2. Wash **beans,** top and tail them, and cut each one into 2 or 3 pieces. Wash and peel **potatoes** and dice them.
3. Bring **3 cups water** to a boil in a heavy pot with a cover. Add **lamb,** cover, and simmer for 30 minutes.
4. Add cut **beans,** diced **potatoes, salt** and **savory.** Bring again to a boil, then reduce to a simmer, cover, and cook until everything is tender.
5. Spoon some of the cooking liquid into a cup and stir in the **flour.** Spoon the mixture into the pot and cook over low heat, stirring until broth is thickened.
6. Add more **seasoning** if needed, and sprinkle with **parsley.**

Pickled Green Beans

preparation time: 15 minutes, plus overnight soaking
cooking time: 25 minutes
makes 4 pints

2 pounds green snap beans
4 tablespoons Kosher salt
ice cubes
2 quarts white vinegar
1 cup sugar
5 garlic cloves
1/4 ounce dried gingerroot
2 tablespoons whole mustard seeds
7 tablespoons dried dillweed

This pickle can be made with dried ginger and dried dill at any season of the year. For even better results, make it in summer when fresh dill sprigs and small, thin, and very fresh beans are available.

1. Wash **beans,** top and tail them, taking off the tiniest piece at each end of the pod, and blanch them in boiling water for 5 minutes. Drain, rinse with cold water, and drain again.
2. Layer **beans** in a large ceramic or glass container, sprinkling each layer with some of the **salt** and adding **ice cubes.** When all are layered in the bowl, pour in cold water to cover. Let the beans soak overnight.
3. Pour **vinegar** into a large enamelware or stainless-steel saucepan. Add **sugar** and stir to dissolve. Peel **garlic** and add, along with **gingerroot, mustard seeds** and 6 tablespoons of the **dillweed.** Bring to a boil and boil for 8 minutes. Meanwhile sterilize 4 pint jars, lids and rubber jar rings.
4. Drain **beans,** rinse lightly with cold water, and put them in an enamelware kettle. Strain the **vinegar** over them. Bring to a simmer and cook for 10 minutes, or until beans are as tender as you like.
5. Drain sterilized jars, set them at an angle, and fill them with **beans,** putting them in so they will be standing upright. Put a scant teaspoon of the remaining **dillweed** on top of each jar. Pour the **vinegar** into the jars to cover the beans. Put rings in place, add lids, and seal. There will be 3 fully packed pint jars; the last jar may not be quite full (eat those beans first). Any leftover spiced vinegar can be used for flavoring salad dressings or for cooking. These taste better well chilled; just before serving, toss them with a little olive oil.

variations: Use 1 ounce of fresh gingerroot instead of dried. Peel it and cut into small pieces. If you can get fresh dill, use 6 heads in the vinegar, and put a few sprigs in each jar before filling it.

Simmered Fresh Shell Beans

preparation time: 10 minutes
cooking time: 15 minutes for
court-bouillon, 15 to 25
minutes for beans
serves 4

1 pound fresh shell beans
1 onion, 3 ounces
3 whole cloves
2 celery ribs with leaves
1 large bay leaf
1 teaspoon salt

Use this basic method for any fresh shell beans, especially if they are to be used already cooked as an ingredient in other dishes or in salads.

1. Pick over **beans** and remove any bits of pod. Peel **onion** and stick with the **cloves.** Wash and dry **celery ribs** and cut each into 3 pieces. Fill a large saucepan with water and add **onion, celery** and **bay leaf.** Bring to a boil and simmer for 15 minutes to make a court-bouillon.
2. Add **beans** and **salt** to the court-bouillon and bring again to a simmer. Cook the beans for 15 to 25 minutes, according to the size of the beans. Drain them.
3. The **onion** and **celery** may be chopped or puréed to add to some mixtures, but most often they are discarded. If beans are to be used in salads, add dressing while they are still warm; they will be more flavorful.

note: If the beans are to be used as a vegetable accompaniment, they may be cooked like Buttered Lima Beans (see Index).

Spanish Bean Soup

preparation time: 20 minutes
cooking time: about 1 hour
serves 6

8 ounces Spanish onions
1 garlic clove
1 pound green peppers
1 pound fresh tomatoes, or 2 cups canned peeled plum tomatoes
4 ounces thick bacon
2 tablespoons olive oil
1 pound fresh shell beans
3 cups water
1/4 cup chopped pitted ripe olives
1/4 cup chopped blanched almonds
1/4 cup chopped parsley

Use any fresh shell beans available to you—cranberry or pinto beans, white or fava beans, or black-eyed peas.

1. Peel and mince **onions.** Peel **garlic.** Peel **green peppers,** or char in the broiler and remove the skins. Discard stems, ribs and seeds, and chop peppers. Wash **tomatoes,** remove cores, and chop (tomatoes can be blanched first if you prefer).
2. Cut **bacon** into 1/2-inch pieces and cook in a heavy kettle until about half cooked. Pour off and discard bacon fat; leave bacon pieces in the kettle and add the **oil.**
3. Put **onions** and **green peppers** into the kettle, and push **garlic** through a press into the mixture. Cook until onions are translucent.
4. Add **shell beans** and stir over moderate heat until beans are coated with fat. Pour in **tomatoes** and **water** and bring to a boil. Simmer for about 1 hour, until beans are tender enough to mash.
5. Stir in **olives, almonds** and **parsley.** Serve in thick bowls with chunks of hearty bread.

variations: The beans can be mashed in the kettle if you prefer a thicker soup. Use a potato masher. Or add about 2 cups cooked rice just before serving, or spoon rice into individual bowls before ladling out the soup.

Rice with Shell Beans

preparation time: 15 minutes
cooking time: 35 to 40 minutes
serves 8

1 pound fresh shell beans (fava beans, cranberry beans, etc.)
salt
2 large leeks
1/2 pound plum tomatoes
2 garlic cloves
3 tablespoons olive oil
1 pound brown rice
juice of 1 lemon
1/2 teaspoon cuminseeds, crushed
2 tablespoons minced fresh coriander

This is adapted from a Lebanese dish.

1. Pick over **beans** and remove any bits of pod. Blanch the beans in ample water with 1/2 teaspoon **salt** for 5 minutes. Drain, rinse with cold water, and drain again.

2. Wash and trim **leeks,** chop them, and wash them again. Blanch and peel **tomatoes** and chop them. Peel **garlic.**

3. Heat **oil** in a large saucepan and sauté **leeks** until golden. Add **tomatoes** and sauté until they are softened. Push **garlic** through a press into the mixture. Add the blanched **beans** and 1 cup **water,** stir well, and cover the pan. Simmer until water is absorbed.

4. Stir in the **rice** and add 3 cups **water,** the **lemon juice,** crushed **cuminseeds,** and 1 teaspoon **salt.** Cover and bring to a boil. Simmer for 15 minutes, until rice and beans are done. If water is absorbed before that, add more, 1/2 cup at a time.

5. When the dish is ready, sprinkle with **coriander,** or stir it in. If you like, stir in a little butter before serving. This is an excellent main dish for vegetarians.

variation: For a more nutritious dish, use chicken stock instead of water.

Hopping John

preparation time: 10 minutes
cooking time: 1-1/2 hours
serves 6

1 pound fresh shell beans (black-eyed peas)
1/2 pound "seasoning meat" (hog jowl or streak lean)
3 quarts water
salt
1 cup polished rice
black pepper
red pepper (cayenne)

This dish is served on New Year's Day in the American South, to bring luck during the year that follows. Every state has its own version.

1. Rinse **black-eyed peas** and remove any bits of pod. Put the **pork** in a large kettle and pour in 2 quarts of the **water** and 1 teaspoon **salt.** Bring to a boil and simmer for 1 hour, skimming as necessary.
2. Add the **peas** to the kettle and simmer for about 25 minutes, until peas are tender. There should be only a small amount of "pot likker" left in the kettle.
3. While peas cook, put **rice** in a separate saucepan and pour in remaining quart of **water.** Add 1 teaspoon **salt.** Bring to a boil and simmer for about 15 minutes, until rice is tender. Pour it through a large strainer, then set the strainer in the saucepan and let rice steam over very low heat until it is dry and fluffy.
4. Mix **peas** and **rice** together in a large serving bowl and stir in enough of the "pot likker" to make the mixture moist. Season with more **salt** if needed, **black pepper** and **red pepper** to taste. Butter is sometimes stirred in also. The seasoning meat can be cut up and served if you like, but often it is not used.

note: Hog jowl and streak lean, from the belly of the pork, are fresh, not cured. However, you will need to order either cut from your butcher unless you live in the South. Lacking these, salt pork or bacon can be used; in that case omit salt.
In South Carolina these fresh beans are called white peas or cowpeas. Many kinds of shell beans are used in other states. Dried peas or beans can be used if fresh shell beans are not available; they need to be soaked overnight. Be sure to simmer the beans, either fresh or dried, so they do not fall apart. The beans are often served without rice, and they bring good luck all by themselves.
Where did the name Hopping John come from? We don't know!

Shrimps, Rice and Black-Eyed Peas

preparation time: 30 minutes
cooking time: about 1 hour
serves 6

8 ounces wild rice
salt
1-1/2 pounds small shrimps
2 tablespoons crab boil
1 pound shelled fresh black-eyed peas
6 ounces white onions
12 ounces green peppers
1 pound plum tomatoes
2 tablespoons peanut oil
2 ounces butter
8 ounces dry white wine
black pepper
2 ounces dry Madeira
1/2 cup salted peanuts

This recipe was an attempt to recreate a dish I once enjoyed at a former rice plantation near Georgetown, South Carolina. Use white or brown rice if you do not have wild rice. Steam rice until tender before proceeding with Step 2.

1. Put **rice** in a large saucepan, cover with boiling water, and let it stand until water is cold. Drain. Pour fresh boiling water over the rice and add 1 teaspoon **salt.** Bring to a simmer and cook for 15 minutes, or until rice is done to your taste. Drain and set aside.
2. Peel **shrimps,** devein them, and rinse. Put them in a saucepan with 2 quarts **water,** the **crab boil** and 1 tablespoon **salt.** Bring to a bare simmer and cook for 3 minutes. Remove from heat and let shrimps cool in the water.
3. Blanch **peas** in ample water with 1/2 teaspoon **salt.** Drain, rinse with cold water, and drain again.
4. Peel and mince **onions.** Wash **peppers,** discard stems, ribs and seeds, and sliver the peppers. Blanch and peel **tomatoes,** and chop them.
5. Heat **peanut oil** and **butter** in a large saucepan. Sauté **onions** until translucent. Add **peppers** and sauté until beginning to brown on the edges. Add chopped **tomatoes** and sauté for 5 minutes, stirring often.
6. Pour in the **white wine** and cook the sauce until somewhat thick. Season with **salt** and **black pepper.**
7. While sauce cooks, drain **shrimps.** Pick off any bits of spices, but do not rinse them for they lose flavor that way. Mix **shrimps** and **black-eyed peas** into the **sauce** and heat.
8. Finally stir in the **rice** and the **Madeira,** and heat. Spoon into a deep serving dish. Chop the **peanuts** and sprinkle around the dish.

Shell Bean Chakee

preparation time: 15 minutes
cooking time: about 30
minutes
serves 6

1-1/2 pounds fresh shell beans
salt
4 slender leeks
1/2 pound fresh cauliflower
1/2 pound butternut squash
2 tablespoons walnut or peanut oil
1/2 teaspoon ground ginger
1/2 teaspoon ground cuminseed
1/2 teaspoon ground turmeric
3/4 cup unroasted cashews
1 cup coconut milk

A <u>chakee</u> is a vegetable curry made of 3 or more vegetables cooked together and flavored with coconut milk and spices. Any kind of shell bean can be used in this, and any yellow squash, even pumpkin.

1. Pick over **beans** and remove any bits of pod. Blanch them in boiling water with 1 teaspoon **salt** for 5 minutes, and drain.
2. Wash and trim **leeks,** cut across into thick rounds, and wash again. Wash **cauliflower** and cut into tiny florets. Peel **squash** and cut into 1-inch chunks.
3. Heat the **nut oil** in a saucepan and stir in the **spices.** Sauté until light brown, then stir in **cashews** and sauté for 2 minutes. Pour in **coconut milk,** heat, and mix. Remove from heat and set aside.
4. Return blanched **shell beans** to their saucepan, add 2 cups **water,** and simmer for 5 minutes. Add **leeks, cauliflower** and **squash,** and simmer until all the vegetables are tender, which should be about 8 minutes longer. Add **salt** to taste.
5. Spoon the **coconut milk, cashews** and **spice mixture** into the vegetables, mix, and simmer for a few minutes longer, until the sauce is somewhat thickened. Do not let the mixture boil after adding coconut milk. If the liquid is not sufficient, add some plain yogurt.
6. Serve hot over rice. Or let vegetables cool to room temperature. This is an excellent vegetarian main dish. As an accompaniment it is very good with fish or poultry.

Fava Beans with Artichokes

preparation time: 20 minutes
cooking time: about 30
minutes, if artichokes and
beans are cooked at the
same time
serves 6 to 8

6 fresh artichokes
3 lemons
salt
6 garlic cloves
1 teaspoon fennel seeds, crushed
1-1/2 pounds shelled fresh fava beans
1 bulb of fresh fennel, with some leaves
3 tablespoons olive oil
pepper
3 egg yolks

A Middle Eastern dish, especially popular in Greece.

1. Wash **artichokes,** peel stems, and cut all the leaf tips. Cut 2 **lemons** into thirds and use one third to rub over the cut edges of each artichoke. Drop artichokes and lemon pieces into a large stainless-steel kettle.
2. Add 2 tablespoons **salt** to the kettle and pour in enough water to cover **artichokes** (they will float, but as they cook they will sink). Peel **garlic cloves** and add to kettle with the **fennel seeds.** Bring to a boil, cover, and simmer for 15 to 20 minutes, until artichokes are just tender. Do not overcook, or they will lose color and flavor.
3. When **artichokes** are done, drain and cool them. Carefully remove all the leaves (save for snacks), scoop out the chokes, and cut stems and artichoke bottoms into small pieces.
4. Pick over **beans** and remove any bits of pod. Simmer in 4 cups water with 1 teaspoon **salt** for about 20 minutes, until beans are tender but not mushy. Pour off and keep 1 cup of the cooking liquid. Drain the beans.
5. Cut off and mince enough **fennel leaves** to measure 1/4 cup. Trim the bulb to the tender center and sliver it. Blanch fennel slivers in a large amount of water with 1/2 teaspoon **salt** for 5 minutes. Drain.
6. Heat **olive oil** in a saucepan and toss **artichoke pieces, beans** and **fennel slivers** in it. Taste and add **salt** and **pepper** if needed. Beat **eggs** with the reserved cup of **bean cooking liquid** and the juice of the remaining **lemon.** Pour this mixture into the vegetables, off the heat, and stir gently to mix. Set over low heat until the sauce is thickened. Garnish with the minced fennel leaves and serve at once.

Fava Beans in Tomato Sauce

preparation time: 30 minutes
cooking time: about 1 hour
serves 8

3 pounds fresh fava beans in pods
1 garlic clove
6 ounces yellow onions
1 large carrot
2 pounds plum tomatoes, or 4 cups canned peeled tomatoes
2 ounces salt pork
1 tablespoon olive oil
1 teaspoon sugar
salt
black pepper
6 tablespoons chopped Italian parsley
2 ounces Romano cheese

1. Shell the **beans;** there should be about 4 cups. Cook them following directions for Simmered Fresh Shell Beans (see Index) for about 20 minutes. Drain the beans, but reserve the court-bouillon.

2. Peel the **garlic** and thread it on a wooden food pick. Peel and mince the **onions.** Wash, scrape, and trim the **carrot,** and chop it. Blanch and peel **tomatoes,** and chop them. (Or drain the canned tomatoes, reserving all the juices, and chop tomatoes.)

3. Blanch **salt pork** for 2 minutes, then drain; chop it. Heat **oil** in a large saucepan and add salt pork. Cook until pork pieces are golden. Drop in the **garlic** and sauté until it begins to brown; discard garlic. Add **onions** and **carrot** and sauté, stirring often, until onions are translucent.

4. Add chopped fresh or canned **tomatoes,** the **sugar,** 1 teaspoon **salt** and a few grinds of **black pepper.** Bring to a simmer and cook until sauce is thick and somewhat reduced. If necessary, add the juice drained from canned tomatoes or some of the strained court-bouillon from cooking the beans. Add more **salt** if needed.

5. Add **beans** to the sauce and continue to cook for 10 minutes longer, or until beans are tender and sauce very thick. Stir in **parsley.** Finally grate the **cheese** and stir it in off the heat.

Broad Beans with Egg Yolks, Cream and Herbs

preparation time: 15 minutes
cooking time: 20 minutes
serves 4

2 pounds fresh broad (fava) beans in pods
3 small shallots
2 ounces unsalted butter
1/4 cup chopped fresh parsley
2 tablespoons chopped fresh mint
1 tablespoon chopped fresh tarragon
2 egg yolks
1/2 cup heavy cream
2 tablespoons lemon juice
salt and pepper

This recipe comes from the British Isles, so we are keeping the name used there for the bean called fava bean in Southern Europe.

1. Shell the **beans.** Peel and mince **shallots.** Melt the **butter** in a heavy saucepan with a tight-fitting cover. Sauté shallots until translucent.
2. Add **beans,** stir them in the butter, and pour in about 1/2 cup **water.** Cover pan tightly and simmer beans over low heat for 10 minutes.
3. Stir in all the **herbs.** If the water is evaporated, add another 1/4 cup. Cover again and simmer for 5 to 10 minutes longer, until beans are tender. Do not let them burn; stir them, and add more water if necessary, but the beans should steam or braise rather than boil so use as little water as possible.
4. Beat **egg yolks** and **cream** together, then add the **lemon juice,** beating all the while. Stir in a ladleful of the **hot beans** to warm the egg yolks, mix well, then turn it all into the saucepan of beans. Gently mix, season to taste, and set over lowest heat (pilot light) until the egg yolk and cream sauce is thickened.

Buttered Lima Beans

preparation time: 15 minutes
cooking time: 15 to 25 minutes
serves 4

2 pounds lima beans in pods
sugar (optional)
2 ounces butter
salt and pepper
4 tablespoons chopped parsley

1. Shell the **beans;** there should be 2-1/2 to 3 cups. Put them in a saucepan and add about 2 cups **water.** The exact amount depends on the volume of the beans and the size of the saucepan. If beans are mature, you may want to add a teaspoon or so of **sugar;** it helps the flavor of older beans. Bring to a boil and simmer for 15 to 25 minutes, according to the size of the individual beans. Test to avoid overcooking.
2. Pour off all but a few tablespoons of the cooking liquid and drop the **butter** into the saucepan. Season with **salt** and **pepper** and shake to mix butter and liquid.
3. At serving time sprinkle with **parsley,** and shake the pan to distribute it.

Succotash—Three Versions

preparation time: about 20 minutes
cooking time: about 20 minutes
serves 6

2 pounds lima beans in pods
6 to 8 ears of fresh corn
1 cup milk or light cream
salt and pepper
2 ounces butter

This truly American dish has an Algonquian name, but it was made all over North America, using different beans in different areas. The first version is found in New England and some of the Middle Atlantic states.

1. Shell the **beans;** measure them. Shuck the ears of **corn** and cut off the kernels. There should be twice as much corn as beans.
2. Cook **lima beans** in 2 cups water for about 10 minutes. Add the **corn kernels** and cook for 3 minutes longer.
3. Pour off most of the cooking liquid and replace it with **milk** or **light cream.** Mix gently and simmer for about 5 minutes, until both beans and corn are tender to your taste. Season, stir in the **butter** and serve as soon as melted.

variations: For a richer dish, use heavy cream. The liquid may be thickened with mixed butter and flour (beurre manié).

DELAWARE SUCCOTASH: Cube 2 ounces of **salt pork** and sauté in a saucepan until lightly browned and crisp. Pour off the fat, but leave the cracklings in the pan. Add **lima beans** and 1 cup water and cook for 10 minutes. Add more water if needed. While beans cook, blanch and peel 8 ounces fresh **tomatoes,** and chop them. When ready to add the **corn,** also add the **tomatoes.** When vegetables are tender, season, and stir in 1 ounce **butter.** Do not use milk or cream in this version.

MEXICAN SUCCOTASH: Peel and chop 3 ounces **onion.** Peel 1 large **red bell pepper** and 1 large **green bell pepper,** or char to remove the skins. Discard stems, ribs and seeds, and chop peppers. Sauté **onion** in 2 tablespoons **corn oil** until translucent. Stir in **lima beans** and 1 cup **water** and cook for 10 minutes. Add more water if needed. Add **corn kernels** and **chopped peppers,** mix gently, and cook until all vegetables are tender. Season to taste. Add a little **butter** if you like.

Lima Bean Purée

preparation time: about 15
minutes
cooking time: about 30
minutes
makes about 3 cups purée

3 pounds lima beans in pods
sugar (optional)
2 tablespoons fresh lemon juice
grated rind of 1 large orange
salt and pepper
3 ounces butter

1. Shell the **beans.** Put them in a saucepan with 3 cups water. Add 2 teaspoons **sugar** if beans are mature (larger and older beans are good for purée). Simmer the beans for 20 to 30 minutes, until very tender.
2. Leave the cooking liquid in the saucepan and with a slotted spoon transfer **beans** to a food mill. Purée the beans into a clean heavy saucepan. If it is too wet or soft, dry it over low heat, stirring almost constantly, until it reaches the consistency you prefer. If the purée is too dry, add some of the cooking liquid, a little at a time, and stir to mix well.
3. Stir in **lemon juice,** grated **orange rind,** and **salt** and **pepper** to taste. Finally mix in the **butter,** stirring it in as it melts.

variations: Omit lemon juice and reduce butter to 1-1/2 ounces. Mix 1/4 cup hot heavy cream into the purée.
For more flavorful beans, cook them with a bouquet garni, or add a minced onion and a bay leaf.
Garnish the purée according to the way you plan to use it—with parsley sprigs or minced parsley, carrot curls, tomato dice, etc. The purée can be used as a garnish; spoon it into hollowed-out vegetables, or pipe it around finished dishes in a green ribbon.

Creamed Flageolets

preparation time: 10 minutes
cooking time: about 25
minutes
serves 6

4 shallots
4 tender celery ribs with leaves
3 ounces unsalted butter
1 pound shelled fresh flageolet beans
1 cup water or chicken stock
1 cup heavy cream
lemon juice
salt and black pepper

If you can find fresh flageolets, use them for this; they are most delicious and the pale green color makes a beautiful dish. However, this recipe can be used for fresh lima beans or other shell beans. Adjust the cooking time according to the bean. Flageolets are quite small.

1. Peel and mince **shallots.** Wash and dry **celery** and carefully remove strings. Cut celery into small slices or slivers.
2. Melt **butter** in a heavy saucepan and sauté **shallots** and **celery** until shallots are translucent. Add **beans** and stir gently until coated with butter. Pour in **water** or **stock** and simmer until all water is evaporated.
3. Pour in **cream** and simmer, stirring now and then, until beans are tender and coated with a thick creamy sauce. Allow about 15 minutes. The sauce must not boil; set the pan on an asbestos pad if necessary to reduce heat.
4. Pour in about 1 tablespoon **lemon juice,** more or less if you like, and season with 1/2 teaspoon **salt** and some **black pepper** from the mill. Serve with lamb, veal, poultry.

Index